CW00820652

CONVERSATIONS

Where *are* we when we read Bollas?
In *Conversations* we may think we are in poems,
or at times theatre pieces, or short essays, but, after
a while, we come to a curious realisation: we have
been put somewhere else. Strangely familiar.
But where? Uncannily, the author keeps the form
a secret until we realise he is staging the world of
inner conversation, which borrows its structure from
human dialogue. Quite a ride this: resonant and
ramifying in its reach.

CONVERSATIONS

Christopher Bollas

KARNAC
firing the mind

First published in 2024 by
Karnac Books Limited
62 Bucknell Road
Bicester
Oxfordshire OX26 2DS

Copyright © 2024 by Christopher Bollas

The right of Christopher Bollas to be identified as the author of this work has
been asserted in accordance with §§ 77 and 78 of the Copyright Design and
Patents Act 1988.

All rights reserved. No part of this publication may be reproduced, stored in
a retrieval system, or transmitted, in any form or by any means, electronic,
mechanical, photocopying, recording, or otherwise, without the prior written
permission of the publisher.

British Library Cataloguing in Publication Data

A C.I.P. for this book is available from the British Library

ISBN-13: 978-1-80013-247-4

Typeset by Medlar Publishing Solutions Pvt Ltd, India

www.firingthemind.com

CONTENTS

BRAND NEW

That's very nice.
Thanks.
Did you buy it round here?
Yes.
Recently?
Yesterday, actually.
So, it's …
Brand new.

Something so nice about new things.
Yes.
You don't know the new.
That's special.

Is it comfortable?
Very.
Comfy and good looking?
Yes, actually.

Did it take long to find it?
Well, I wasn't actually looking for it.

You weren't looking for it?
No, just happened upon it.

My God, were you lucky.
That's what I thought.
You must have been so surprised.
I was actually.

Bowled over?
What?
Did you almost feel bowled over?
I wouldn't go that far.

I would have been.
Yes?
For sure.
Well it's a find.

I would have gone all dizzy.
Really?
All light-headed and faint-like.
That's something.

And that's not usual for me.
Really?
No. Not usual at all. But if I had seen it …
You would have nearly fainted?

How about that?
Yeah.
That's really something.
It sure is.

So, I am really lucky.
You are?
It might have killed me seeing it.
My God.

Yeah, that could have been a problem.
You can say that again.
So, I'm glad you have them.
I can see that.

Well …
Oh.
Come back any time.
Sure.

CAN I HELP YOU?

If I can help let me know.
Sure.
Sometimes it's just nice to look.
True.

Without knowing what you are even
    looking for.
Right.
As you see we have many different
    kinds here.
Yes.

Do you have any particular favourites?
Not really.
It takes time.
Yes.

Take your time.
Thanks.
I'm not following you, but it helps
    if I walk around.
Oh.

It gets tiring standing on one's feet all day.
Of course.
I also get a bit lonely.
Ah.

Talking helps to ease that.
I see.
Yes, walking and talking, and talking
    and walking.
Um.

Rather like you, but you are looking
    and walking.
Well.
But you won't be here long and I will.
Yes.

So we are not in the same position.
I suppose that's true.
We are in the same place but not the
    same position.
Um.

If I were you coming across me I wouldn't
    want to talk.
Well, I uh.
Some of us come across as too aggressive.
Um.

Poor taste.
I agree.
But I like your taste.
Thanks.

Your outfit matches some of our stuff.
Well, I wasn't quite thinking along
    those lines.
For someone else, then?
I hadn't reached that point.

A truly free looker, then.
I suppose so.
Looking, just looking, not even knowing
    why or for whom.
A bit aimless?

No, you're a free spirit.
Oh.
Absolutely. Imagine my position here.
What?

If I were free I would run like hell.
You look at these all day long.
To the point of madness.
Oh dear.

But I watch those who are looking.
Yes?
People look differently.
They look differently or they look
    differently?

Both.
Ah.
No two people look alike and no two
    people look alike.
That's interesting.

It stems the madness of the invariable
    objects before me.
Makes sense.
You look in a very particular way.
I do?

Yes.
What do I look like?
Like someone who wonders whether
    to buy or shoplift.
What?

It's just your impression.
I look like a thief?
No, you look like a thief.
That's what I said.

That's not what I meant.
But it's what you said.
Some sayings have many meanings.
Oh.

The fact that you look like a thief, does
    not mean you look like a thief.
I will try to remember that.
I thought for a moment you were going
    to steal that one over there.
Where?

The one on the third shelf, four over.
Third shelf, four over?
Yes.
Gosh.
What?
I own that already.
You do?
Yes.

So, I was wrong. You look like an owner.
I see.
A man who already owns things and does
    not need to look.
I look like I don't need to look?

That must be it, don't you think?
Well, but exactly why?
Because you told me.
What did I tell you?

That you already own it, so you have the
    look of an owner.
Oh, I get it.
Tricky isn't it?
It sure is.

Well …
I have to move on …
Yes of course.
Nice talking to you.

IT FEELS GOOD

It's kind of nice doing this.
I agree.
What's special about it for you?
That's hard to answer.

I know.
That's part of why it's so wonderful,
    do you agree?
Oh yes, absolutely.
Would you say it's the sense-side of it?

Yes and no.
What's the yes side of it?
The sensations are so intense.
Absolutely.

And unexpected.
You mean, exciting because not
    anticipated?
Yes, there is a surprise element to it.
It's always like the first time.

Yes, that's right.
The emotion of it all.
Is it the same for both of us?
Hard to say.

Hard to know.
I can't know your inner experience.
Nor I yours.
But it's emotional.

For sure.
Is it like anything?
Kinda like swimming in some
    strange sea.
My word.

What?
I had that image.
You did?
When you said kinda, I saw the sea.

That's amazing.
You know, we come from the sea.
Not us personally.
No, but our species did.

That's true.
Yes.
Interesting, isn't it.
Maybe it's a foretelling.

What?
Perhaps it points towards something.
It indicates something?
Taken all together, yes.

You think it's incremental?
Additive?
Could that be?
Suppose so.

It's a form of knowledge.
Yeah, a kind of knowing.

Most would not think of it as a learning
	experience!
Oh heavens, no.

They would laugh, if we put it like that.
Or worse.
We could be driven out.
Exactly.

Because they might think we were
	spoiling it.
By trying to figure out how it all works.
Yes, by atomising it.
Fragmenting it into tiny bits.

That idea would be wrong, however.
Because we are not doing that.
Definitely not.
Just trying to share an experience, yes?

Yes, trying to put the hard-to-word
    into words.
And it is so special.
That maybe … what do you think?
Maybe we should, you know.

Give up talking about it?
Yeah.
Yeah, that's not a bad idea.
So, what else interests you?

CUSTOMER RELATIONS

I work in customer relations.
I completed my training two years ago.
So I am rather fresh, so to speak.
But it is challenging.

My family asked, why do this?
They hate customers.
I understand.
As customers, they were always
    treated badly.

So I told them, well, I want to make
    things better.
For whom? they asked.
In all sincerity I said for the customer.
So that is how I began.

But I must say.
Customers can be difficult.
Like today.
I had a challenge.

A well-dressed man, much better off than
    me, rang the bell.
I was there in a flash, as I am supposed
    to be.
He stared at me without speaking.
I asked if I could be of help.

He remained silent.
I must say, it was a bit different.
I had not been trained for him.
So I was unable to enact my procedure.

He said that we had cheated him.
I asked in what way.
He said that he could not remember.
He handed me a receipt.

I told him it would be hard to help.
He asked why.
I said because he could not remember.
But we had the slip.

I looked at it.

It said Tyson cook-pot.

The price was $29.95.

I asked if he was unhappy with the Tyson.

He said he could not remember.

I said may I wonder out loud?

He said, ok.

I said, if he could not remember, why was
he here?

He stared at me again without speaking.

Two, three, perhaps five, minutes passed.

I was challenged by this.

He did not change.

Finally he spoke.

He said I remember.

I was so relieved.

What did he remember?

He said he remembered his father.
I was taken aback.
He looked at me with a deep gaze.
I did not know what to say.

He then said that his father hated banks.
I was silent.
He then said that his father hated credit.
I was silent.

He looked at me.
I looked back.
Our eyes met in some place I had never
    been before.
We understood something, without
    knowing.

He said he had to have his money back.
I asked why.
He said it had not worked.
I asked, in what way?

He said that he had never been
    understood.
I said that was sad.
He said he had only just realised this.
I said that must be a relief.

There was a silence.
People behind him swiveled their heads
    to look.
I did not know what to say.
My colleagues pushed the "help" buttons.

He said he had come to return the
    Tyson pot.
I jumped in. I said because he had
    been misled.
He looked at me, moving his head from
    left to right, from right to left.
He said, yes, that was exactly right.

I said I would refund him the money.
He said thank you.
I said it was the least I could do.
He said it was more than he expected.

SHOPPING

SHOPPING

Glad to get you.

What?

Where are you going?

I was on my way to the store …

Were you walking or driving?

I was walking. I like the exercise.

So you weren't going to buy much?

Not a car-load, no. I like the daily shop.

Isn't it cheaper to buy in the supermarket?

I like supporting the locals.

You think they are local?

Of course.

In what sense?

They are in my locality. My area. I can
walk.

So you are taken in by that nonsense,
are you?

Nonsense?

They are not local.

What, are you being aggressive? You are
kidding? What is this?

They are all part of a wide chain of global
     marketing.
The locals?
An illusion.
Well, if so, I should have been dining
     on illusions.
You seem content with that idea.
That's one way to lose weight.
But you seem more than hefty.
So, you are giving up on this silly idea
     of yours.
No, you like illusions.
Oh come on, give this up.
You buy globalised.
What does that mean?
Your local is simply an atomisation
     of globalisation.
Get out of here.
It plays on sentiment.
What sentiment?
You think it is sweet to shop at your local.
     It makes you feel good.

I am supporting my community.
No, you are paying more to make yourself
    feel like a good guy.
I know my butcher and fishmonger are
    not part of a chain.
How do you know that?
They would have given it away.
You think they are dumb?
Of course not.
Good. Now you are wisening up.
To what?
To the fact that they are not simple little
    independent cuties.
What is this?
I think you should knock this off.
What?
These sentimental strolls through your
    little utopia.
I think you are astonishingly cynical.
No, informed.
I think you are plain wrong.
Then ask your local guys.

No.

Because you are afraid.

No, it would be rude.

They might be cross with you.

I don't know. Possibly.

You would not want to ruin your quaint
presence in the village.

I don't need to ask them.

And why?

Because I know they are authentic.

What epistemology serves you with the
authentic?

I just know.

Oh, the old gut feeling.

Perhaps.

You think in your belly.

I would not put it that way.

Belly brains.

You know, I really don't like this.

Go on, ask them.

No.

Coward.

No.
Ignorance is your bliss.
Just a minute.
Yes?
Who the hell are you?
None of your business.

MEMORIES ARE MADE OF THIS

I am not sure about memory.
It seems a dangerous game to play.
It can be so easy.
You can have it your own way.

No one to say no.
No one to say that is not quite right.
No one to say you have it in reverse.
No one to say it never happened.

I am not sure about memory.
It can be dismissed.
Maybe nothing ever happened.
So something is amiss.

But I do believe in who I was.
The me that did my remembering.
The me that said I won't forget this.
The me that saw the future to find
    my past.

Memory is dangerous.
It can play you about.
It is a form of bliss, so alluring
    it takes over where mother left off.

Am I right?
Is it not the case that I saw a rope hanging
    in the haunted house?
Was there not blood on that rope?
Did we not call the police?

Memory.
I saw the girl in the street as we ran
    into her.
Slow motion.
She lived, right?

Memory, you are only concerned with
    yourself.
Those of us who have to go beyond you
    feel your pull.

A tug of war.
You usually win.

But I knew your tug of love.
You taught me early on.
I could live inside you.
And never be released.

So I fought you, didn't I?
I fought and fought and fought.
I created a false history.
To defy you.

I lived inside your nemesis.
Fantasy took you over.
I did you in.
You were too painful.

But I am old now.
I have time for you.
I don't have much to lose.
And you know this.

So you are slowly coming back.
In bits and pieces.
Sometimes in a jolt.
A real bolt from the blue.

You had me last night.
The wave was 30′, my father was on the
    beach, waving his arms.
My friends were alarmed.
I took off on a wave that could kill me.

I woke and said, what a dream.
Later in the day, memory came.
It was true.
I put a call in that night.

You remember that day?
How could he forget, he said.
He thought he would never see me again.
I said I thought I might have imagined it.

He laughed.
Memory laughed with him.
I was relieved.
Memories are made of this.

ON BOARD

OR SEATO

Pardon me.
That's ok.
There is so little space.
That's for sure.

Do you mind if …
No problem, let me do it.
That's very kind of you.
Once you're stuck-in, it's
    difficult to move again.
I know.

They don't really give a shit, do they?
I reckon not.
We shouldn't have to live in these
    conditions.

Nope.
It's just for the money, don't you think?
Yeah.
Are you reading something?

I'm sorry?
What are you reading?
A novel, a very long one.
That's lucky.

Yeah.
I will leave you alone, then.
Uh …
I'm ok.

That's good.

READING

READING

You are reading.
Yes.
Awful?
I agree.
Same old thing, day in day out.
Depressing.
If it isn't one thing it's another.
Um.
Nothing good left.
That hits the nail on the head.
Why do we still bother?
Self mutilation?
Brilliant metaphor.
Thanks.
You know what?
No.
I'm going to give it up.
Like a bad habit?
Like any bad habit.
Why should we read when it isn't worth it?
After all, what's in it for us now?

We don't learn anything.

That's for sure.

We submit ourselves to the same daily
    torture.

I couldn't agree more.

Who said that those who fail to study
    history repeat it?

I can't remember.

Well, we read about it day after day.

We are informed.

It's hardly the case that we are not studious.

But look at the results.

Yes, fat lot of good it has done us.

Indeed.

Ok, I've decided.

Me too.

If we've started something, at least we
    won't know.

That's right, isn't it.

Because we won't read about it.

What a brilliant conversation.

A great relief.

LOOKING THROUGH
THE WINDOW

There I was
looking at the butcher's display
all those great pieces
of meat.

Rack of lamb
fillets of beef, pork loin
venison and
chickens cut into all shapes.

There
standing and looking
gazing at the
sight.

I heard a voice next to me.
A boy.
He said, Mum, what has happened
to the animal?

I heard the mother's laugh.
The way a mother laughs

at these sorts of childish
questions.

She told him this was the butchers
and he said, Mum, the animal has
    exploded.
And the Mum laughed her anxiety, and
    tugged him
away from further questions.

The word exploded and laminated
    itself on
the butcher's window and
every time I passed by, I saw it
and sometimes I saw Iraq.

I like the butcher.
We are friends.
But so is the fishmonger.
So I went there instead.

I went to the fishmongers for weeks
    on end.
I avoided the butcher until
eventually I went.
Crossed through the word and
    entered Iraq.

THE OVERALL SITUATION

It's rather confusing, don't you think?

Sorry?

The situation we are in.

What situation?

The whole thing.

Oh.

Yes.

Well.

I shouldn't let it get to me.

No.

Occasionally it just hits.

Um.

Everything has gone belly up.

Belly up?

How to put it?

Don't know.

Speaking is a problem.

Um.

Hard to put it into something sensible.

Yes.

We can't say "it will all get better some day".

No.

Just won't do.
No.
Were all sort of …
Screwed.
Yes.
Fucked.
Is that all we can say?
Ah.
You see my point?
Yes.
How to put it?
Is it … necessary?
Well, it's personal really.
Personal?
Saying "fuck" doesn't really do it.
Right.
You think that?
"Fuck?"

Yes.
Sort of.
What do you think?

With the "F" word?
Yes.
It goes "fuck this shit".
You add "shit?"
I add shit.
It's not good is it, really?
It doesn't speak to things.
The overall situation.
No.
Can we think of something to say?
What?
The two of us.
But.
A sentence or two.
To help ourselves?
To protest.
To dissent.
Something cogent.
Cogent?
Powerful word, that.
Sounds like a cleanser.
"Cogent".

If we could say something cogent …

Easier said than done.

Is "Fuck" cogent?

Well … I don't know really.

Maybe it's a good starting point.

It's used a lot.

True.

We should come up with something
memorable.

I think you've hit it.

Words that sum it all up.

Words we can be proud of.

Even if we are fucked?

Absolutely.

Even if the situation is beyond and we
have no clue?

Well, we don't do we?

So … anything occur to you?

An odd thing.

Go for it.

An image of a demented bee.

An image of a demented bee?

Yes.

What does it look like?

It ignores plants and suckles shoelaces.

You saw this?

No, it popped into mind.

Shoe laces?

From one person to another, going all
around.

What is this?

I read it.

Bees suckling shoelaces?

Bees going crazy.

What kind of crazy?

Losing it.

Like.

Dying off, confused.

Shit.

Yes.

Serious shit.

That's why it came to mind.

How do we work with that?

We have to come up with something.

Seems urgent.

We can be activist.

Verbal ones.

It's all that's left to us.

So.

Well, can you try?

Ok.

You look like you have something.

"Bees don't suck; we're fucked".

Wow.

I know.

That's it.

Good.

We've done something.

Against our situation.

Yeah.

Protested.

Hope to see you again.

Yeah, who knows?

That's true enough.

We know that much, right?

For sure.

WHAT IS HAPPENING?

What's happened?
I'm not sure.
Do they know how it started?
They don't say.
We don't know how it began?
Or what it is.
Or what to do about it.
Did they seem frightened?
I wouldn't say that.
What then?
Bewildered. They looked bewildered.
Do you think it looks bad?
Hard to say.
We don't even know what it is.
Or what to do about it.
Could be harmless.
Not so sure.
Why not?
Their faces.
Bewilderment?
Stumped.

If it was harmless what would we see?
Good question.
Not knowing is upsetting.
True.
So what should we do?
Nothing.
We can't figure it out.
For sure.
That's for them.
Absolutely.
Should we stick around?
We should go?
Yes.
Where?
Just away?
It could be in other places.
Have you heard anything?
No.
Would we have heard something?
Don't know.
They may not wish for word to spread.
Yes.

It could create panic.

Well, maybe.

Wouldn't it?

But if it is good.

People might be full of hope?

Yes.

It could be some kind of religious thing?

Religious?

Like God arriving?

That would be something.

Umm.

Or God could have sent us something.

Could have.

If it was from God and not from
    elsewhere.

Elsewhere?

What if it is from Mars?

Shit.

If they had bad intentions.

Dreadful.

If they had good feelings.

Then it could be some kind of outreach
    programme?
It might be.
So this thing is not from our planet?
We seem to think that.
We might be out on a limb with that.
Yes, it's rather wild thinking.
We should probably cool it.
Fortunately we are not in charge.
True.
We could have spread panic.
Thinking out loud can be dangerous.
Keep our thoughts to ourselves.
Mum's the word.
I sure do wonder what it is though.
So do I.
But we have to leave it at that.
I think so.
Whatever it is, we will find out.
Umm, something will emerge.
Eventually.
In time.

DO I LOOK STUPID?

Mind if I ask a question?
A question?
Simple but important.
Is this a survey?

Of sorts.
I don't have time for surveys.
It's not an official survey.
You are not working for someone?

Yes, but not to administer a survey.
Whose survey is this then?
Mine.
A private poll?

Yes.
You have a licence?
What?
To survey.

I have to have a licence?
Of course you do.

To ask a simple question?
You should be wearing a lanyard.

What?
An identification tag.
But my question is only for you.
What?

I only thought of asking this question
    just now.
You mean this isn't a survey?
No.
Then why did you say it was?

I can't remember. I am rather confused.
Do you see this?
Your watch?
Yes.

Why am I looking at your watch?
Because you have two minutes and then
    I am off.

So, I can ask a question?
Get on with it.

Do I look stupid?
What?
Do I look stupid?
What do you mean do you look stupid?

When looking at me do you see a stupid-
    looking guy?
I don't know how to answer that question.
Why?
Because it's absurd.

To wonder if I look stupid?
Yes.
But if I do can you see how awful this
    would be?
What?

If I look stupid I suffer, don't I?
How?

Because people would avoid me.
But not everyone is the same.

Some would not think that I look stupid?
How would I know?
So you do think I look stupid.
I didn't say that.

It's implicit in what you just said.
For a man who thinks he looks stupid,
    you seem bizarrely complex.
But that's the horror.
What?

If you look stupid, no matter how clever
    you might be, it's all over.
What do you mean, it's all over.
People would never take me seriously.
I have to go.

You promised to answer my question.
I did.

No. You said you could not answer
   the question.
Well, that was my answer.

But that leaves me hanging.
It's an honest answer.
It's evasive.
What?

You dodged the question.
I don't like the question.
Ah.
What do you mean Ah?

That seems more to the point.
I'm glad to please you.
You won't answer the question because
   you don't like it.
That's right.

That's unfortunate for me.
Why?

Because asking it risks much of my soul.
What are you talking about?

I told myself, go on, ask someone and
    I did.
Well, so what?
Having suffered this view all my life, at
    last I asked someone.
That's not my fault. I did not ask for this
    question.

But once asked, you knew its importance.
I thought it idiotic.
It came from my soul.
Well complain to your bloody soul.

It was the result of decades of hard inner
    work.
To ask this dumb question?
To end my agony.
At my expense?

It had to be a stranger, no one who
    knew me.
Why?
To get an honest answer, not sympathy.
I'm sorry I failed you.

You can remedy this.
How?
Please answer the question.
You mean, you want a definite yes or no.

That's right.
You want me to say whether you *look*
    stupid.

That's absolutely right.
And when I answer this question?

I promise I won't say anything.
You will let me get on my way.

I will forever be in your debt and yes you
    can go right on your way.
Are you sure of this?

I swear to it.
Ok then.
Well?
You look stupid.

ALONG CAME A SPIDER

Sorry to intrude.
Well, I am rather …
I think I should …
As you can see I am …

Into your work, but
If you don't mind …
You have a large spider on you.
WHAT!

A large spider.
OH MY GOD, WHERE IS IT?
On the back of your jacket.
OH MY GOD. HELP. PLEASE HELP ME
    SOMEBODY.

I don't think running around will help.
OH GOD. HELP. HELP.
People are worried.
GET OFF OF ME. GET OFF ME.

They don't know who you are referring to.
OFF, OFF, OFF.
Taking your jacket off hasn't worked,
    I'm afraid.
WHERE IS IT?

It's hard to tell with you standing on your
    head, but I think
        WHERE, JUST TELL ME WHERE.
It travelled up your pant leg.
OH JESUS. OH LORD. HELP ME
    PLEASE.

People are very alarmed.
OH MERCY. MERCY.
Taking your trousers off isn't a good idea.
WHERE IS IT?

I see it.
WHERE?
Sit down please.
OHHHHHHHHHHHHH.

Stay still.
DO YOU SEE IT?
Oh for God's sake.
WHAT!

Silly me.
What?
I am so sorry. It's a piece of black fluff.
Black fluff?

Doesn't that look like a spider?
You idiot.
I was trying to help.
You put me through …

Why don't you pick up your clothes.
I cannot believe this.
That's a good idea.
What have you done?

I believed in what I saw.
I was in your hands.

What?
Your perception was my fate!

I thought I saw a spider.
You drove me mad.
It could have been a spider.
I followed a delusion.

THE MAN WITH NO WORRIES

Whew, all that rain.
Um.
What a mess.
I suppose.

Nothing bothers you?
Not really.
Nothing?
I wouldn't say nothing.

What then?
My appearance.
Your appearance?
How I look.

Look?
How I look on the day.
On the day?
Whether I fit in or not.

Fit in?
It's just a feeling.

You said nothing worries you, but this
    is huge.
That's an exaggeration.

I'm glad I don't have that worry.
I didn't until you asked your question.
It's my fault?
I hadn't thought of it.

It's as if you don't exist.
What?
How would you know how to fit in the
    world?
On the day?

On the day.
By looking.
At what?
At myself.

How would that tell you anything?
I would get a feeling.

Of what?
Whether I looked right or not.

But what would determine that feeling?
I don't know. It just happens.
This means there is no you that knows
    yourself.
How do you get that?

You rely upon a feeling rather than your
    self.
What?
You worry about how you appear?
I've admitted that.

But if you knew who you were that would
    not matter.
What?
How you appeared would be irrelevant.
Why?

Because you could only appear as
    yourself.
Not always.
There are exceptions?
I look different from day to day.
You look different?
I look in the mirror and I do not look
    the same.
You look like someone else?
I look different.

There are many of you?
I have different ways of appearing.
Are we talking hair styles, pimples,
    puffy skin?
No. I look in the mirror and I see
    difference.

What kind of difference?
I don't always look the same.
So you do not have a self.
I feel I do.

That's no good.
Why not?
You are so many selves, you cannot
    possibly be a self.
Is that a problem?

Well, you wouldn't want that to get
    around now, would you?
Why?
It means you have no identity.
What is that, anyway?

Identity?
You have the answers.
It's your mark.
My mark?

You are identifiable.
Identity is the identifiable?
Of course.
I'm identifiable.

You've just said you are not.
What?
You said you have too many appearances.
It's still me.

How could you be identifiable if you
    appear so differently so often?
Well, I know who I am.
How is that possible?
Just because.
Even though you dress to fit in with
    the world?
Yes.
Even though you give yourself up in order
    to fit in?
I don't give myself up.

Well, if you kept your self, wouldn't it
    always appear the same each day?
Well.
Yes, well.
Why are you making so much of this?

Because you said nothing worries you.

So?

Well, it should, because you really do
not exist.

I certainly do. Who do you see when you
see me?

A guy.

Well.

So what?

Well, that means I exist.

I mean you have no self.

But I still exist.

But if you have no self, even though you
exist, you are not really here.

What?

A scarecrow exists but it has no self.

You think I look like a scarecrow?

You might as well be one.

That's a hell of a thing to say.

Yes.
No, really. That hurts.
Ok.
It has upset me.

Oh well, forget it.
I can't.
Try.
I'm trying.

Ok?
Man, what a way to begin the day.
Don't worry about it.
I'll try.
Good.
Not sure about this.
Who is?
Oh.

WHAT IS IT?

Pardon me.
Sorry?
I don't mean to break in.
Well.

I've seen something.
Seen something?
I can point it out.
You can?

Yes.
Where is it?
Over there.
I'm looking.

See it?
No.
Up a little.
Oh.

See that?
Yes.

What is it?
No idea.

Seen anything like it?
No.
Neither have I.
What do you think?

It's rather odd.
Disturbing.
Should we do something?
Like what?

Tell people?
Tell them what?
I don't know.
That's the problem.

We could be in danger.
I say.
Right.
We should warn the others.

Absolutely.
What if it is there to protect us?
Telling could be a serious mistake.
People might panic and destroy it.

We would no longer be protected.
This is a dilemma.
Should we put it to the vote?
How could we do that without telling?

We vote and see who wins.
There are only two of us.
We could both vote yes to tell.
Or no not to tell.

If it's a true vote, it has to be by secret
    ballot.
I agree.
I have paper and pencil.
So how about "yes" to tell and "no"
    not to tell.

Sounds good.
Finished?
Yes.
Let's look.

Well?
One yes, one no.
Oh crap.
Deadlocked.

What do we do?
There must be a procedure.
Yes, must be.
We can't be the only ones who have been
    here before.

That must be true.
What do you think others have done?
We should know.
It's in our genes.

An instinct.
Gut feeling.
Have you got one?
Yes. And you?

Yes.
What do we do?
Is your gut feeling complex?
I can put it into one word.

Me too.
Great.
Let's write and see what we come up with.
Done.

Same here.
What is written?
"Nothing".
"Nothing"?

We both wrote "nothing".
Astonishing.

Indeed.
That's it then.

We followed procedure.
Ancestral.
Yes.
Upheld things.

CYBERSPACE

"Cyberspace" originally appeared in
The Psychoanalytic Review,
Volume 94, Issue 1, February 2007.
https://doi.org/10.1521/prev.2007.94.1.7
https://guilfordjournals.com/toc/prev/94/1

Is this seat taken?

No.

May I sit down?

Sure.

Is that interesting?

Well …

Cyberspace, huh?

Yes.

Ever wondered if we were in it?

I beg your pardon.

Do you think we are, you know, inside it?

Literally?

Well, we wouldn't know, would we?

We wouldn't know what?

We wouldn't know we were inside it
    or not.

Why not?

That tree over there could be a
    cyber-image.

I don't think so.

But you can't say you know this for sure.

I have no problem saying I know it
     for sure.
A man with no doubt?
I didn't say that.
Well how can you be certain we are not
     cyber-figures?
I would know by now.
How would you know?
I would have found out.
How?
I think this is a silly conversation.
Actually, it is rather philosophical.
Well, I have never liked philosophy.
So, you wouldn't even care to know if you
     actually exist or not.
I didn't say that.
But if you decline philosophy you aren't
     really equipped to think this out.
That's nonsense.
Well, what form of knowledge do you use
     to think?
My intuition.

What's that?

My sense of things.

Your sense of things?

Yes.

What if your sense of things was that you
were an onion.

What?

What if you felt you were an onion?

That's preposterous.

No, it's simply evidence of an intuition.

But it's stupid.

But if you were an onion it would
be correct.

But I am not an onion.

How do you know you are not an onion?

Because I don't feel like one.

How would you know how it felt to be
an onion?

Because if I were an onion I would know.

You are claiming that an onion
is conscious of itself?

I didn't say that.

Well you did.
No I did not.
I'm sorry, but you said you would know
    if you were an onion.
I would feel it.
How could you feel you were an onion
    without thinking?
Maybe I would bring tears to my eyes.
No, I think you would bring tears
    to my eyes.
If I were an onion, I would be a human
    onion.
A human onion?
Of course.
How could you be both human and
    an onion at the same time?
Well you brought up cyberspace.
And?
I could be both a human and a cyber-
    creation at the same time.
I don't think so.
Why not?

Because that's not possible.

I thought anything was possible.

Where did you get an idea like that?

Well, why not?

That's irresponsible thinking.

I thought you were a philosopher.

I'm not, but what has that to do with this?

You chastened me for not liking
     philosophy.

Because one must think about some
     questions through philosophy.

So, isn't this a philosophical question?

It is not proper philosophy.

Why not?

It's just a loose idea.

What is that?

It's an idea without thought.

How is that possible?

It hasn't been thought through.

Why is it not a thought?

To qualify as a thought it has to go
     through thinking.

How do you know this?

My training.

As what?

I am a thinker.

How do you know that?

It comes with being me.

And me?

You disown philosophy.

You said you are not a philosopher.

But I believe in it.

So what?

If you believe in something it
    licenses you.

To do what?

In my case, to be a thinker.

That's crazy.

If you believe you are an onion you have
    certain licences.

Such as?

You could claim vegetable knowledge.

What is that?

It is the knowledge vegetables possess.

But they don't think!
Not like you or I, but they think
    vegetably.
Why would I want to think like
    a vegetable?
It would bring you certain advantages.
Such as?
Much of the earth is vegetation.
What could I do with this knowledge?
You could vegetate.
That's a curse.
You don't appreciate the art of vegetation?
You are diminishing me.
To vegetate is to meditate.
Vegetation meditation?
Like Zen works for people.
I'm a floor potato?
If you got into vegetation.
Is this a cyberspace discussion?
It could be.
Because I don't feel there is anything real
    about this.

I don't think y shou wor y.
What is happening?
Th th ng a out cy sp ce.
What is happening to your wording?
I be ve t at I m y
What is happening to your nose?
I do t wa t t
You are disappearing.
Hello?
Hello?

ON THE SAME PAGE

I've no idea where I am.
Where you are?
Did someone say something?
Me. I've no idea where I am either.

Do you feel anything?
Yeah.
What's it like?
Like being inside a page …

A book?
Don't know. Could be anywhere
    in the print world.
Where are you on the page?
I can't figure it out. My senses don't get it.

I can't feel my place either.
At least we are on the same page, don't
    you think?

Wait till we get turned over.
Um.

Yes?
I think we are being watched.

SELF WITH OTHER

Self: Alright?
Other: Kind of you to ask.
Self: Sure thing.
Other: And you?

Self: Yeah. Fine.
Other: I love that word.
Self: Which one?
Other: Fine.

Self: Yeah?
Other: Makes me feel good.
Self: The word?
Other: Oh yes.

Self: Do other words do that?
Other: I can't think so clearly now.
Self: Sorry, I asked too much.
Other: That's ok.

Self: Are you feeling ok with what I said?
Other: I am a little hurt.

Self: Oh dear.
Other: Don't worry.

Self: I didn't mean it.
Other: I know.
Self: Can I help?
Other: Can you pass me the empathy?

Self: Oh, good, I've lots!
Other: Thank God for empathy.
Self: Yes and it's not so expensive.
Other: Really?

Self: I can get it at Walmart for
    half price.
Other: Half price?
Self: Yeah.
Other: Blimey.

Other: Where can I find it?
Self: Housewares.

Other: Housewares?
Self: Next to the Teflon pans.

Other: Teflon?
Self: I was surprised too.
Other: How do you figure?
Self: They told me empathy is cheap
    and doesn't stick.

SHOULD WE ENTER?

You are reading *The Guardian*.

Uh?

The Guardian.

Yes.

Interesting?

What?

Anything of interest?

Oh, well.

I know.

Hard to say.

So much has happened.

And so little.

True.

Um.

I do think, however, we face an inevitable question.

Inevitable?

Should we have entered?

You mean.

Yes. Did we have the right?

The right. That's strange.

Strange?

It never occurred to me.
Whether we had the right?
No. I mean the phrase.
"Did we have the right?"
Yes, that's it.
You hadn't thought of this?
Well, I had.
But not put like this.
Yes, that's it.
What do you think?
I like it.
Like it?
I love the phrase.
"Did we have the right?"
Yes, it's an arrow.
Goes to the heart?
Yes.
Well, do you?
No.
No?
Well, what is right?
Right is what one sees as being it.

Being right.

Of course.

God, isn't it good.

To be right?

No, to feel it.

Um.

A rush.

If you feel it.

Poor buggers who don't feel it.

What if you feel it is wrong?

Oh.

Rather different.

Completely.

What is the difference?

Well, you shrivel up if it's wrong.

No rush.

No, a pruning up.

Pruning up?

Faces go all prune-like.

Disapproval?

Terrible facial effect.

Christ.

Awful isn't it?
You enter, you get a rush.
You defer, you become a prune.
God.
I know.
So.
Always enter.
Even if we …
No even ifs.
But if it's wrong?
No, come on, you have to enter.
What of the consequences?
What?
The consequences.
What consequences?
The after-effects.
Should be ok.
What?
You got to go for it.
But why?
The rush.
Like any fucking.

Like fucking?
How can you know until you are inside?
Maybe it looks bad.
Ugly even.
So?
Still, could be a great entry.
How great?
Lots of ugly situations are fantastic
    upon entry.
But the signs were terrible.
I'm not so sure.
What?
Think of it.
Of what?
Entry into WMD!
What's that?
Well, we all know.
We do?
Sure.
What is it?
"Women of Mass Delivery".
Oh my God.

So.

That's why we went in?

Well?

Kind of a no brainer?

Glad to hear you say that.

But it's been devastation.

Great, yes?

I, no, I don't think so.

What, a pussy?

Sorry?

You a pussy?

That means, exactly …

A cunt.

No.

No what?

I'm no pussy.

So entry is good.

Entry where?

Into any pussy.

You think it was pussy?

What else?

And.

If you're a man, you enter pussy.

Oh.

You get it.

Um.

Can't wait for the next entry.

That's *The Guardian* you're reading?

Shit.

What?

Couldn't find *The Sun*.

Oh.

Well.

Cheers then.

Yes, cheers.

THE DELAY

God this is boring.
All this waiting.
What do you suppose is wrong?
I've no idea.

Must be some reason for this delay.
I would have thought so.
Do you suppose something has
    happened?
Possibly.

Maybe it's always like this?
I don't know really.
That would be quite strange,
    don't you think?
It sure would.

People would be upset on a regular basis.
I would have thought so.
I think I would have heard about it.
Yes.

Do you think you would have heard
     about it?
I don't know.
Do you know how much time has passed?
No.

That's odd, neither do I.
Strange.
I suppose it's because we didn't know we
     would have to wait so long.
We didn't look at our watches to start
     counting.

I never looked at my watch.
Neither have I.
We have no idea how long we have
     been here.
True.

It has to be a very long time.
Quite.

At least hours.
Perhaps.

Sometimes twenty minutes can feel
    like five hours.
If bored.
And we are bored.
Yes this is tedious.

Nothing is happening.
Not to my knowledge.
I can't see any movement.
Neither can I.

So we may not have been here all
    that long.
It's possible.
They say that time flies.
Not here.

No, not here.
What would we say about time here?

Grounded?
That's pretty good.

Time grounded.
We are grounded.
No.
What?

They say time stands still.
Yes that's true.
Is that accurate for our waiting?
I don't know.

When time stands still I think it means
    things are interesting.
Something is fascinating.
Things are timeless.
Here we are burdened by time.

Yes.
It has slowed down.

To a crawl.
Still no movement.

That is right.
Are we in a philosophical problem?
What?
A philosophical dilemma?

How?
Our sense of time is bound to this space.
I had not thought of that.
Neither had I until now.

What does it mean?
Well, I'm not sure.
I know that I don't know.
Maybe it means that some spaces give
    off a different time sense.

Is that possible?
Waiting in Casualty might take one hour
    but feel like five.

Um.
Going for a fun ride is short because
    delightful.

So where we are has its own time to it?
Maybe.
Um.
Does philosophy help?

It doesn't make our situation any better.
We are still stuck.
Still no movement.
It's worse because we don't know why.

That's it, isn't it?
If we knew why, we would not feel
    so stuck.
It's the not knowing.
So this is not about time, it's about
    knowledge.

Yes, it's about not knowing where we are.
Um.
Right?
Absolutely.

Well?
Guess we just have to wait.
Like all the others.
What a bore.

A THOUGHT SEARCHING
FOR A THINKER

I'm a thought.
What kind?
Looking for a Thinker.
I'm a Thinker.

My lucky day.
Not necessarily.
There's a price?
Not any thought has my services.

I might not be worthy enough?
Unlikely.
How would I know?
I ask questions.

Ok.
Where are you from?
I don't know.
Good.

Good?
If you were an American thought, that
    would be in my face.
And?
America is beyond thinking.

Its thoughts cannot find a Thinker?
Bushwhacked.
W?
The one who ended thinking.

Oh.
So, thought, what are you?
A question.
Shoot.

Was it right to invade Iraq?
That's you?
Yes.
You want me to take you on?

Yes.
Why?
Because I cause trouble whenever I seek
    a Thinker.
No doubt.

You know something?
You may be passé.
I need to have a Thinker.
So what?

I get released.
From?
From those who tried to think me
    without being true Thinkers.
Imposters?

I found out the hard way.
That's a problem being a thought without
    a Thinker.
Rumsfeld & Cheney seemed real.
Real?

I know I was in their mind.
How do you know?
I was tortured.
That's them.

Exploited me.
You were had.
I had not been with Thinkers.
And W?

They told me, never, ever approach him.
Because?
He cannot bear to think.
Bad for a thought in need of thinking.

I was in the middle of a lot of shit.
Of course.
Being this thought was a trauma.
And?

Some imposter said I was there to get
    rid of WMD.
Who?
Too many for me. I needed someone
    to think, like you.
And?

I was used.
How?
Manhandled.
You know this?

They spoke in many languages.
Oh.
With bizarre feelings.
Bizarre?

Some felt safe with me, others that I was
    murderous.
You needed a Thinker.
I did! I did!
You were too much trouble for a Thinker.

That's my experience.
I can't take you on.
Why?
Too much.

Like what?
Thinking you through.
Why?
The consequences.

For whom?
For me.
And me?
No problem, you are simply
    a passing idea.

That's my fear.
Naturally.
That is why I am here.
Sure.

It's a terrible fate to be discarded.
The best thoughts have been.
Why the problem with me?
Easy.

Sounds good and bad.
It is.
What is easy?
Most everyone knows the answer.

They do?
They always did.
The problem?
The people.

That sounds like a lot of support.
Yes, but they are silenced.
Is that bad?
Depends.

My fate hangs on it?
Sorry, no.

It doesn't?
Your time came, went, now it is too late.

Me?
You ask whether Iraq should have
    been invaded.
You won't take me on?
There is no point.

Why? You could re-present me to the
    world. You could extend me.
Well ordinarily that is my job.
My friends in the art world are usually
    welcome.
You exist in the world of international
    politics.

Is that bad?
As far as Thought goes, fatal.
I cannot find a Thinker?
Not a qualified one.

What do I do?
Just exist as is.
A thought with no Thinker?
Yes.

This is terrible.
There is some hope.
Yes?
Historians.

Are they Thinkers?
One day they may agree to take you on.
Because there is no risk?
They exist because they live without fear.

Without fear?
The players are all dead.
No consequences?
You got it.

How long do I have to wait?
Well, don't be taken in by elections.

No I have been there. I have been
	hijacked!
Yes, it's easy to abuse you.

No qualified Thinker would do that.
No, but you will have to wait.
For what?
For someone who seeks you out,
	who encourages you.

It will be a feeling?
Yes, you will feel someone earnestly
	seeking to think you.
Are you sure?
Yes.

How do I know this to be true?
Well, you are a sexy thought, aren't you?
Yes, unfortunately.
So money could be made of thinking you.

I guess so.
So by refusing to take you on …
You are not trying to cash in on me.
Correct.

But some other Thinker will, some say.
No, he will lose.
What?
Qualified Thinkers always lose.

So I have to wait for a loser?
Yes, and that will be your gain.
A qualified loser is hard to find.
Try Vegas.

BEING AND NOTHINGNESS

1

Nothingness: Where have you been?
Being: The usual place.
Nothingness: Was I missed?
Being: Some asked why is Being without
Nothingness?

2

Nothingness: You like being yourself?
Being: I don't give it much thought.
Nothingness: You don't give being much
thought?
Being: I don't need to.

Nothingness: If I were you, I would give
myself a lot of thought.
Being: If I were Nothingness, I would
think that way too.
Being: Did you know that people are
afraid of you?

Nothingness: Of me?

Being: Quite a few, actually. It takes up
a lot of my time.

Nothingness: That's rather silly, isn't it?

Being: Not if you were Being.

Nothingness: What is there to fear, then?

Being: Try death.

Nothingness: That is such crap.

Being: Crap?

Nothingness: I have nothing to do
with death.

Being: But death is Nothingness, isn't it?

Nothingness: I look dead to you?

Being: No.

Nothingness: So there is nothing to
the fear.

Being: I shall have to think about this.

Nothingness: Think?

3

Nothingness: Do you enjoy celebrity?
Being: What are you talking about?
Nothingness: You are everywhere.
Being: Is this your envy again?

Nothingness: No. Look at Hamlet. "To be or not to be, that is the question".
Being: What has that got to do with anything?
Nothingness: He doesn't say "To be nothing or not to be nothing" does he?
Being: No, but Trump said that.

Nothingness: He did?
Being: It scared the shit out of him.
Nothing: Got him moving?
Being: Sure did.

Nothingness: So I can be of some use.
Being: Lots of people get moving because of you.

Nothingness: I wish I could think about that.
Being: No worry. I think about it all the time.

Nothingness: Pass on the occasional thought?
Being: Depends on whether we are in America or not.
Nothingness: Why?
Being: Can't be done in America now.

4

Nothingness: Did you say anything?
Being: What?
Nothingness: Did you say something, or were you just thinking?
Being: I was just thinking. You are also a celebrity.

Nothingness. How?

Being: You are in *Lear*: "Nothing will come of nothing".

Nothingness: Oh, thanks a lot.

Being: Well, you feature big there.

Nothingness: It's a put-down.

Being: No, I think it is very clever.

Nothingness: It means I am not creative, and nothing will come out of me.

Being: But if nothing comes out of nothing, then more nothingness has been created.

Nothingness: That's interesting.

Being: See, I told you there is nothing to worry about.

Nothingness: I wish I could think like you.

Being: It's no big deal. Think nothing of it.

5

Nothingness: Being?
Being: Yes?
Nothingness: Why do I know I exist?
Being: Because I am here.

Nothingness: And if you were gone?
Being: You would not know of your
   existence.
Nothingness: Why is that?
Being: Because without Being there is no
   Nothingness.

Nothingness: So I am your dependent?
Being: We are co-dependents.
Nothingness: We need each other?
Being: We cannot exist without one
   another.

Nothingness: So there is no Being
   without Nothingness?
Being: So I have been told.

Nothingness: How does that figure?
Being: Without Nothingness I would not
    stand out.

Nothingness: I am a backdrop?
Being: Yes.
Nothingness: Second fiddle?
Being: An important fiddle.

Nothingness: Who told you this?
Being: It could have been any of a number
    of thinkers.
Nothingness: Like who?
Being: Maybe Heidegger or Bob Dylan.

6

Nothingness: What does it feel like
    to be you?
Being: Full.
Nothingness: Full of what?
Being: Full of myself.

Nothingness: What does it include?
Being: Everything.
Nothingness: Do you include me?
Being: I had not thought of that.

Nothingness: Because if so, then I am
    inside you.
Being: You might be.
Nothingness: Do I only exist inside you?
Being: No, you are everywhere.

Nothingness: Omnipotent?
Being: No. You are without power.
Nothingness: Do you have power?
Being: I may think I do.

Nothingness: But not actually?
Being: No.
Nothingness: Are you everywhere?
Being: No.

Nothingness: So am I larger than you?
Being: Yes.
Nothingness: Do I outlast you?
Being: You were here before me and will
    be here after I am gone.

Nothingness: Will I know that?
Being. Not sure.
Nothingness: Why?
Being: Because you are Nothing
    without me.

7

Nothingness: Who creates war?
Being: We both do.
Nothingness: Do I start it?
Being. No, I do.
Nothingness: How do you do it?
Being: When I assume the other is
    nothing compared to my Being.

Nothingness: The other?
Being: Actually, the object.

Nothingness: What's the difference?
Being: The object is the other after you
have taken its place.
Nothingness. Is it fun?
Being: Very.

Nothingness: What is fun about it?
Being: I get to destroy the other.
Nothingness: But isn't the other a form
of your Being.
Being: Yes.

Nothingness: So, doesn't that destroy Being?
Being: That's the pleasure.
Nothingness: What's pleasing?
Being: I get to offload excess Being.

Nothingness: You lose weight?
Being: Yes and you gain.

Nothingness: So, there is something in it
for me?
Being: Without war you would only be
empty.

Nothingness: I would not want that.
Being: No, of course not.
Nothingness: Empty is just you without
me.
Being: Exactly.

Nothingness: So we need war.
Being: If fills our coffers.
Nothingness: Oh
Being: Hum

8

Nothingness: Something was said in
your name.
Being: Yes?

Nothingness: About the unbearable
    lightness of being.
Being: So?

Nothingness: I thought you were heavy.
Being: Most think so.
Nothingness: But someone thought
    otherwise.
Being: It happens.

Nothingness: Why would someone find
    you light?
Being: Because of you.
Nothingness: Me?
Being: Of course.

Nothingness: You know I cannot think.
Being: Yes.
Nothingness: So, what does this mean?
Being: It means that I cannot be carried,
    as I am too light.

Nothingness: Not heavy enough?

Being: No, I am too light under the circumstances.

Nothingness: What circumstances?

Being: You.

Nothingness: How do I bear on this matter?

Being: Any being, knowing of you, finds being painfully light.

Nothingness: Why?

Being: Because any one's being is distressingly short.

Nothing: Is this my fault?

Being: I am not sure.

Nothing: You who do all the thinking are not sure?

Being: I think about it a lot.

Nothingness: What is there about me that
    causes this pain?
Being: Few know who you are.
Nothingness: But all come from me.
Being: And all end with you.

Nothingness: Doesn't that suggest to you
    that I am known?
Being: It permeates me.
Nothingness: I permeate you?
Being: Yes.

Nothingness: A while back, I thought I
    was inside you.
Being: True, but I am also inside you.
Nothingness: So you come from me?
Being: No.

Nothingness: But selves think so.
Being: Some do.
Nothingness: Others don't.
Being: Where do they come from?

Being: God

Nothingness: Oh shit, not Him again.

Being: He is quite popular.

Nothingness: He is a pain in the ass.

Being: I suppose he takes much of your business.

Nothingness: Until the very end.

Being: The very end?

Nothingness: They look for Him. They find me.

9

Nothingness: Are you thinking something?

Being: Always.

Nothingness: Can you spare me a thought?

Being: Humans are shit.

Nothingness: Where does that put me?

Being: In the shithouse.

Nothingness: Not unless I choose to be there.

Being: You have no choice.

Nothingness: I always have a choice.

Being: I don't think so.

Nothingness: I can be nothing at any moment.

Being: And therefore you stand out.

Nothingness: When was the last time I stood out?

Being: At a high school parade in Iowa when no one showed up.

Nothingness: Was I bad?

Being: You were terrific.

Nothingness: Did people worry?

Being: They weren't there to worry.

Nothingness: How about the Beings who were there?

Being: I took a lot of shit for this.

Nothingness: Doesn't that piss you off?

Being: Why should I answer Nothingness with a substantive remark?

Nothingness: I love allowing it to disappear.

Being: Well, screw you.

Nothingness: If I were inseminated by you, what would that be?

Being: If Being screwed Nothingness?

Nothingness: Yes, what would we create?

Being: It's called America.

Nothingness: I have heard you moan about this often.

Being: Not sexual moaning.

Nothingness: But we were talking about
screwing.
Being: Yeah, but I was fucked.

Nothingness: Did I play a part in this?
Being: That goes without saying.
Nothingness: What did I do?
Being: I have no idea.

Nothingness: You have no idea what part
I played in America?
Being: No, at first you were a slight
outbreak.
Nothingness: And?
Being: I was occupied.

Nothingness: What occupied you?
Being: Existentialism.
Nothingness: Oh, I love that time!
Being: Yes, we were together then.

Nothingness: So how did we drift apart?
Being: You were becoming a country.
Nothingness: Without my knowledge?
Being: No. Without my knowledge.

Nothingness: Is there a solution?
Being: Not in the near future.
Nothingness: When then?
Being: Look, when I say America, you
    take over.

SO I WENT DOWN TO SHOP

So I went on down to shop.
Not for anything in particular.
Looking around.
Saw lots of people.

They were all shapes and sizes.
Men and women.
Different colours.
A few Americans I think.

I'm not sure why I went.
It was good to get out.
But then I didn't know where to go.
So I kept moving down the high street.

I went into a record store.
There were thousands of records.
Maybe more. Maybe a million.
A sea of music, all stored up.

I was confused by it all.
I wanted so many different recordings.

All that Mozart. So much Mozart.
Everywhere.
So I left empty-handed.

I walked on.
Nowhere in particular.
I had a coffee, even though I didn't
    want one.
But I had to sit down.

But then I had to clear out.
So I kept on walking.
My feet were hurting.
I bumped into a large woman.

She yelled at me.
Something like, you dumb fuck.
I was sorry, but couldn't speak.
So I hurried it up a bit.

I walked into a kitchen store.
It was like a material lunatic asylum.

Everything seemed razor sharp.
Dangerous, on the loose.

I hated it there.
Didn't remind me of food at all.
So I left.
I kept walking.

I stepped into a puddle of water.
My shoes were soaked.
I squeaked as I walked.
I didn't know what to do.

So I went into a large department store.
I went up the escalator, all the way
    to the top.
I was in furnishings and sat in a chair.
It was wonderful.

I stayed in furnishings for a long time.
I took off my shoes.

I rung out my socks.
I could have stayed the night there.

But a store person came and asked if
    I could be helped.
He stared at my feet.
I apologised.
I went down the escalator.

When I got onto the High Street it was
    dark.
I was disorientated.
The coffee was not sitting well in me.
I thought I should try to eat something.

I found a pizza parlour.
I ordered a pepperoni pizza with extra
    cheese.
I wolfed it down.
It burned the hell out of the roof of my
    mouth.

I was back on the street and my mouth
	was killing me.
I remembered an article about hot food
	and mouth cancer.
I wondered if this meal would be fatal.
I decided to go home.

I got on a bus.
It was the wrong bus.
Going in the wrong direction.
It did not stop for a very long time.

I spent hours trying to find a bus that
	would go my way.
I found a stop that listed a bus going
	my way.
It took an hour for it to come.
It was such a relief to be going in the right
	direction.

I got off the bus.
I waited for another connection.

It started to rain.
I did not have an umbrella.

I waited for thirty minutes before the
    bus came.
The driver said the bus would terminate
    at the next stop.
I was upset, but it was no use.
I was the only passenger.

The next stop had no connections to any
    bus that would go in my direction.
I did not know what to do.
I saw a coffee shop across the street.
I went in and ordered a cup of tea.

The tea made my mouth burn again.
I decided to walk home.
It was four or five miles.
So I left soon and walked.

I walked and I walked.
I walked and never looked up.
I only ever looked at the ground.
I did not want to know how far from
    home I was.

It was now very late.
Past my ordinary bedtime.
I lost one of my shoes.
It got stuck under a slab of concrete
    on the pathway.

I took off the other shoe.
I walked in my socks
I kept walking.
It was now midnight.

I saw my home.
I was so happy.
I reached into my pocket.
I grabbed my keys.

My keys went flying.
I watched them.
A perfect arc
Disappearing down the drains.